THE BROONS GUIDE TAE

Etiquette and Good Manners

THE BROONS GUIDE TAE
Etiquette and Good Manners

BLACK & WHITE PUBLISHING

First published 2017
by Black & White Publishing Ltd
104 Commercial Street, Edinburgh, EH6 6NF

1 3 5 7 9 10 8 6 4 2   17 18 19 20

ISBN: 978 1 910230 47 3

Text by Euan Kerr and Black & White Publishing
www.thebroons.com

A CIP catalogue record for this book is available from the British Library.

Typeset by Creative Link, North Berwick
Printed and bound by Opolgraf, Poland

Good manners cost nothing. Or so they say, but for a very reasonable price, you can learn the Broons' secrets of Etiquette and Good Manners. Unless, of course, you're reading it for free in your local book shop. Tut tut! Poor etiquette indeed! You need the Broon family's help . . .

In no circumstances should mature gentlemen wear garish or outlandish clothing. This merely draws attention to one's lack of good taste and draws ridicule. Badly fitting clothing is also to be discouraged. Always dress appropriately.

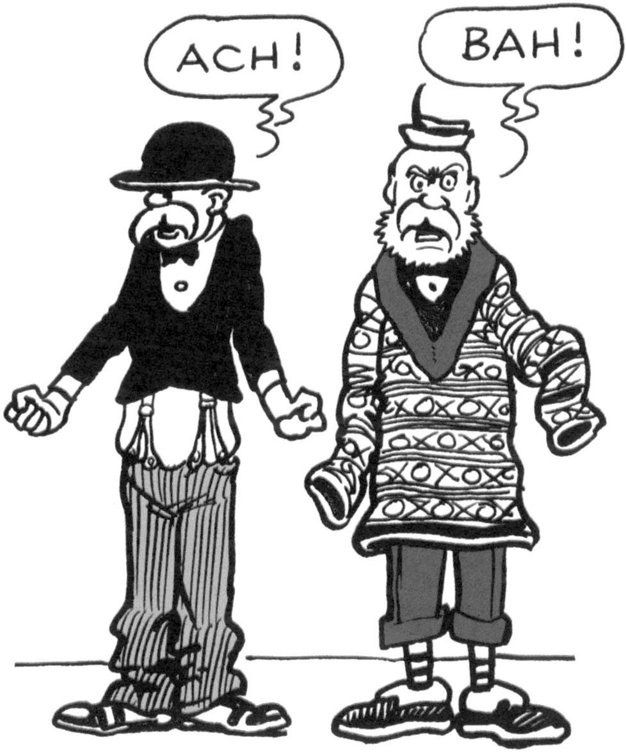
ACH!
BAH!

After a long walk on a warm day, it is considered poor form to stick one's perspiring feet in one's refrigerator to cool them down. This is neither hygienic nor polite and can also result in severe frostbite should one lapse into slumber.

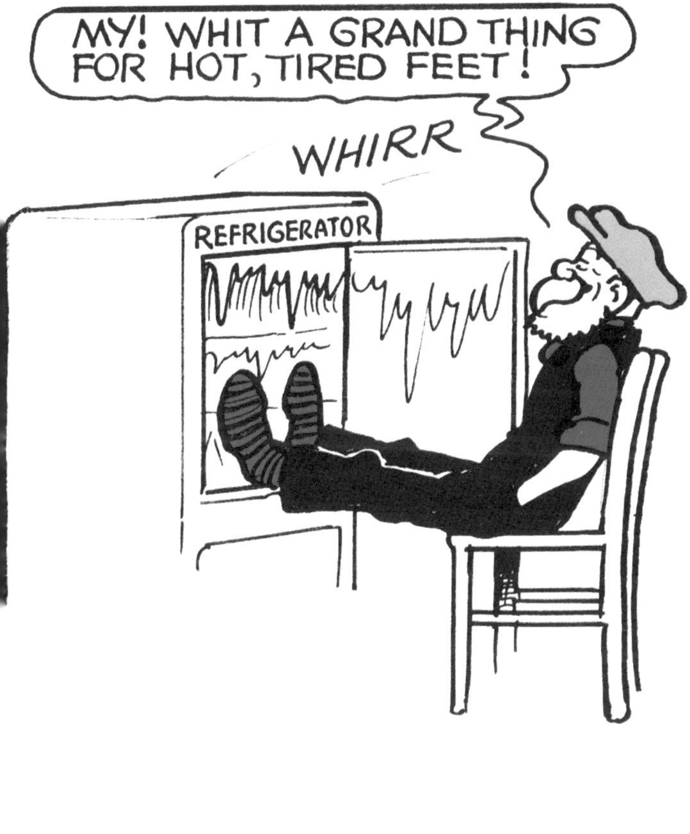
MY! WHIT A GRAND THING FOR HOT, TIRED FEET!
WHIRR
REFRIGERATOR

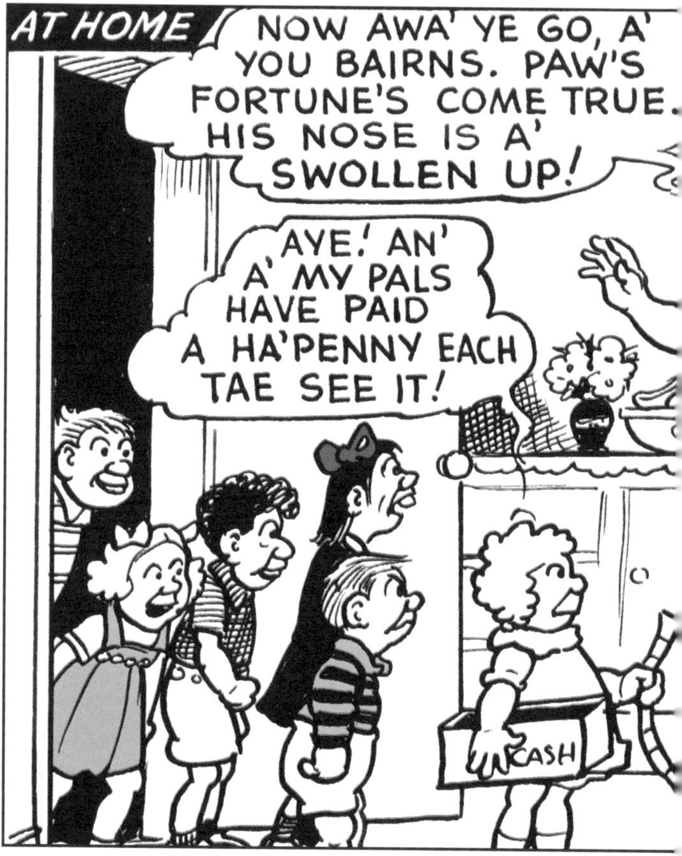
AT HOME
NOW AWA' YE GO, A' YOU BAIRNS. PAW'S FORTUNE'S COME TRUE. HIS NOSE IS A' SWOLLEN UP!
AYE! AN' A' MY PALS HAVE PAID A HA'PENNY EACH TAE SEE IT!
CASH

It is the height of bad manners to mock or ridicule a poor chap's physical afflictions. This even applies when it is

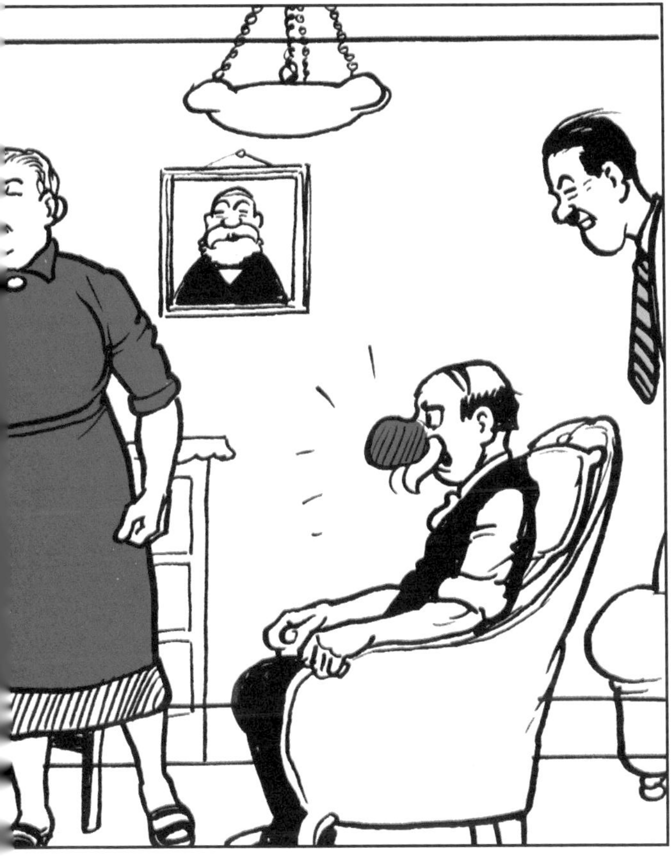

one's foolish, old father and his swollen proboscis is absolutely hilarious!

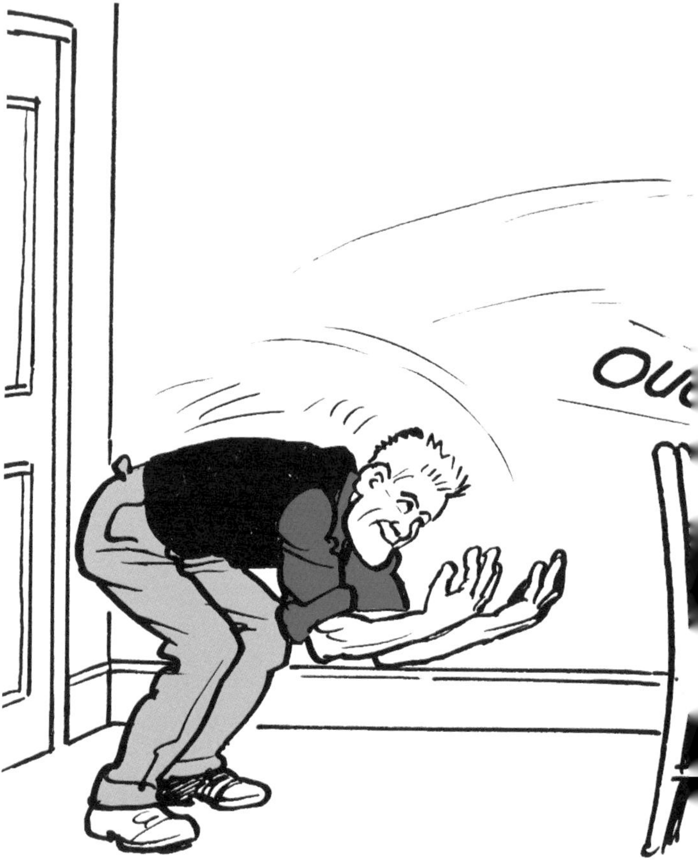

Re-enacting WWF wrestling moves in the confines of the home are both dangerous and lacking in consideration. It can

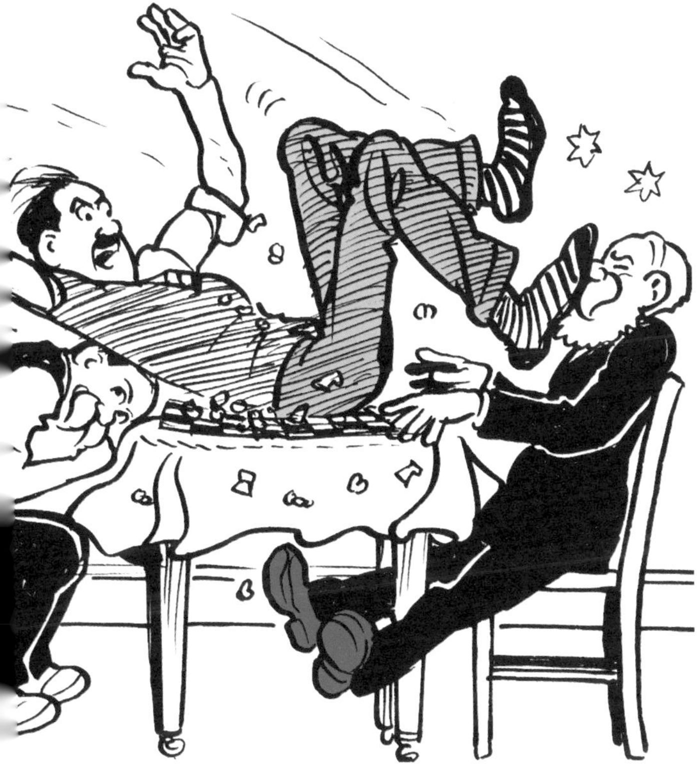

lead to injury and upset. Kicking one's grandfather in the face is also deplorable etiquette.

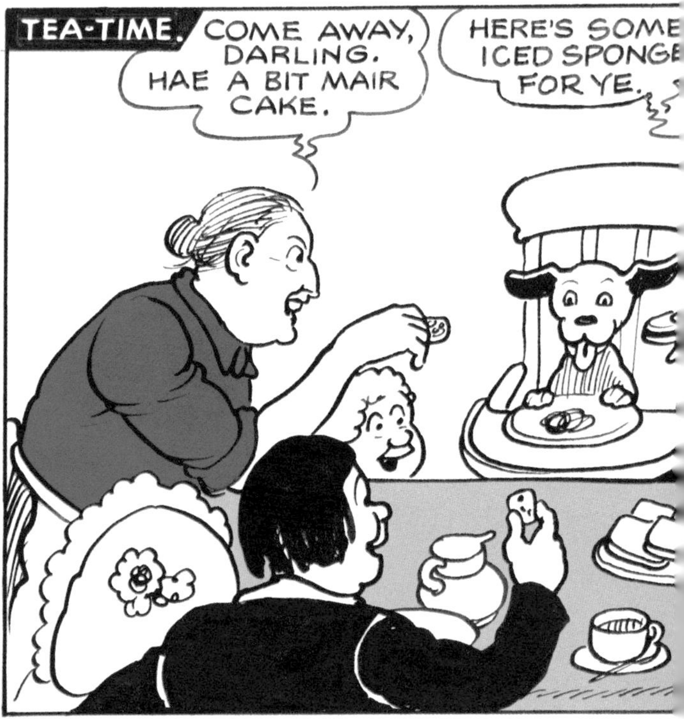
TEA-TIME.
COME AWAY, DARLING. HAE A BIT MAIR CAKE.
HERE'S SOME ICED SPONGE FOR YE.

Maternal older ladies and unmarried spinsters should be discouraged from treating pets as substitute children.

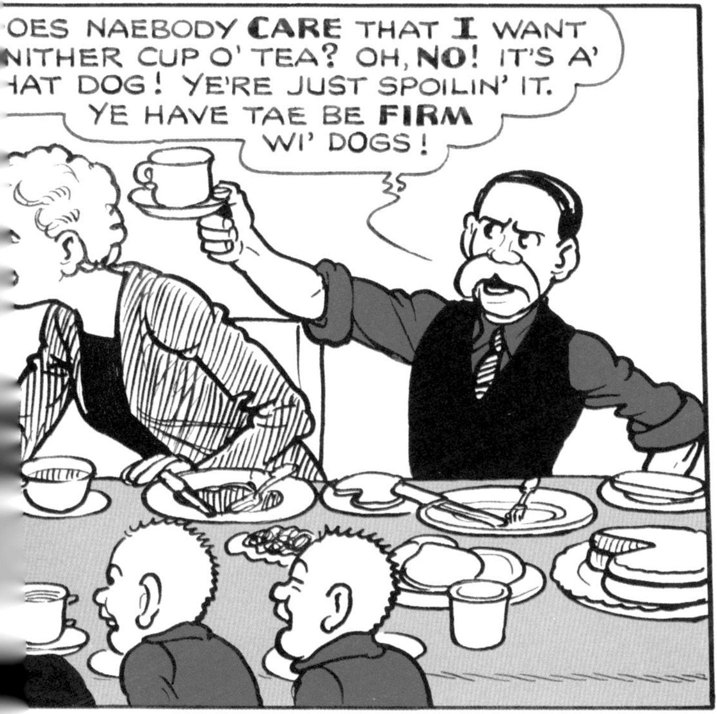
OES NAEBODY CARE THAT I WANT
NITHER CUP O' TEA? OH, NO! IT'S A'
HAT DOG! YE'RE JUST SPOILIN' IT.
YE HAVE TAE BE FIRM
WI' DOGS!

Nor should they ignore the needs and sensibilities of the head of the household.

Standing directly in front of a roaring fire is rude and dangerous. Not only does it block the heat from the rest of the household but the smell of well-cooked posterior is similar to that of sizzling bacon and makes everyone feel exceptionally hungry. Oh, and one's 'breeks' may catch fire!

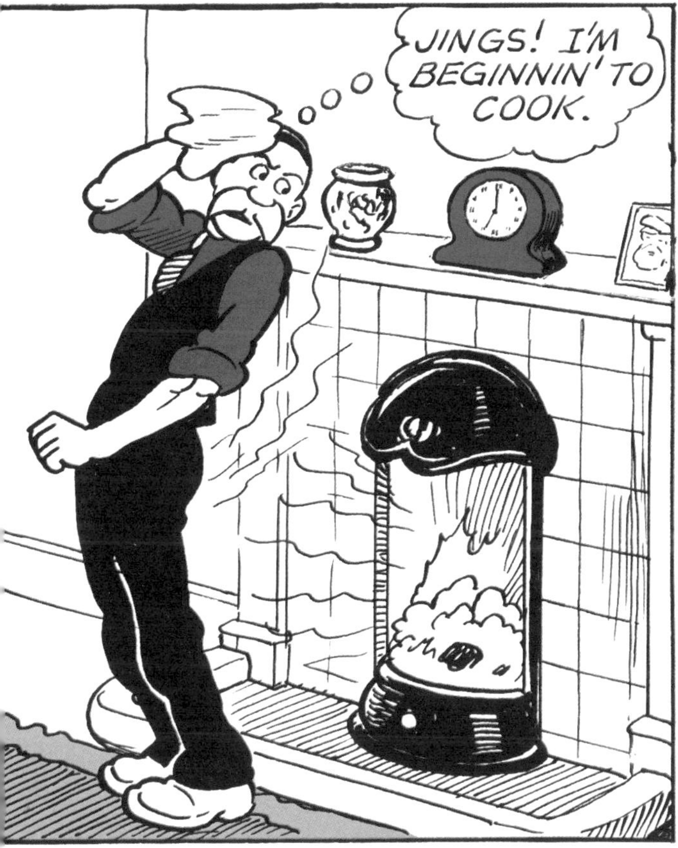
JINGS! I'M BEGINNIN' TO COOK.

When coughing or sneezing, it is good manners to cover one's mouth and nose with a clean handkerchief. Otherwise one's cheese-and-onion snacks may end up decorating the carpet. As the proletariat say, 'Don't be manky – use a hanky!'

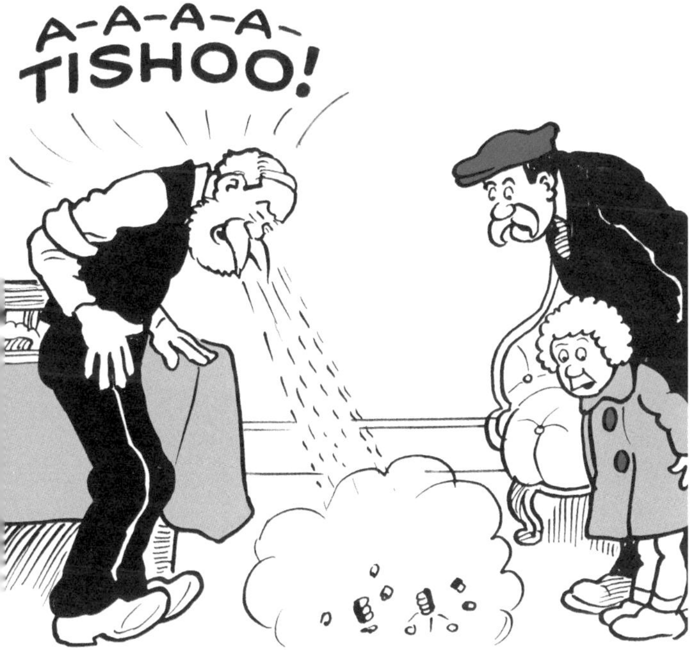
A-A-A-A-
TISHOO!

Hungry children – be warned! No matter how starving you might be, it is not acceptable to scrounge for crumbs or tit-bits in the folds of a gentleman's trouser.

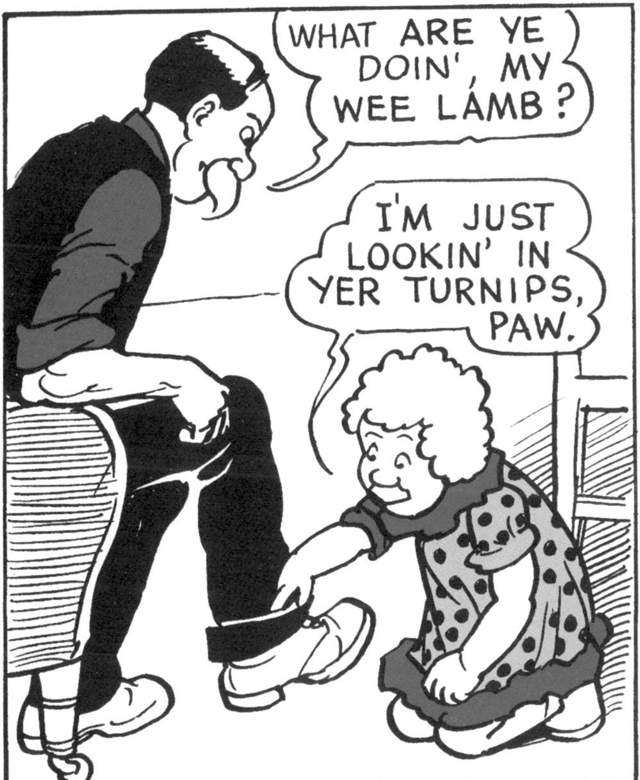
WHAT ARE YE DOIN', MY WEE LÁMB?
I'M JUST LOOKIN' IN YER TURNIPS, PAW.

No matter how irritating a younger sibling might be, it is never permissible to try to insert his head up his bottom. It can cause severe pain and may distress observers.

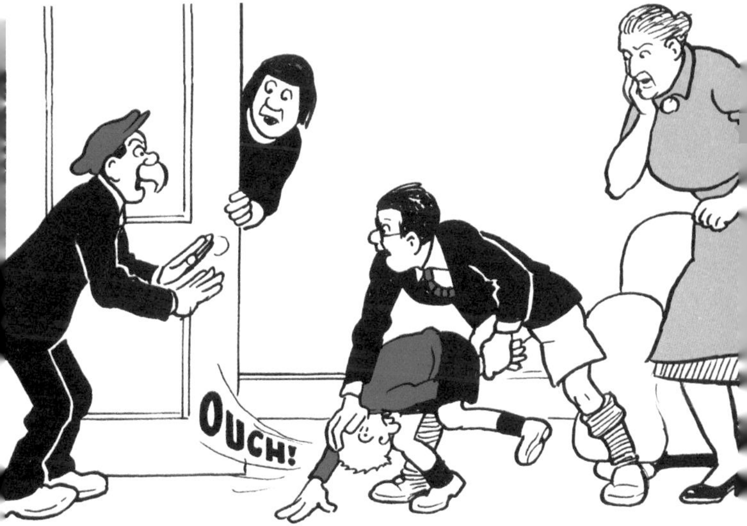
OUCH!

In games of Hide-and-Go-Seek, etiquette demands that contestants never share the same hiding place. This is really a child's game in any case and more mature participants merely look foolish.

A loaf of bread is not a suitable anniversary present — especially for one's long-suffering spouse. No matter how much she may seem to appreciate the gift, it's simply not on!

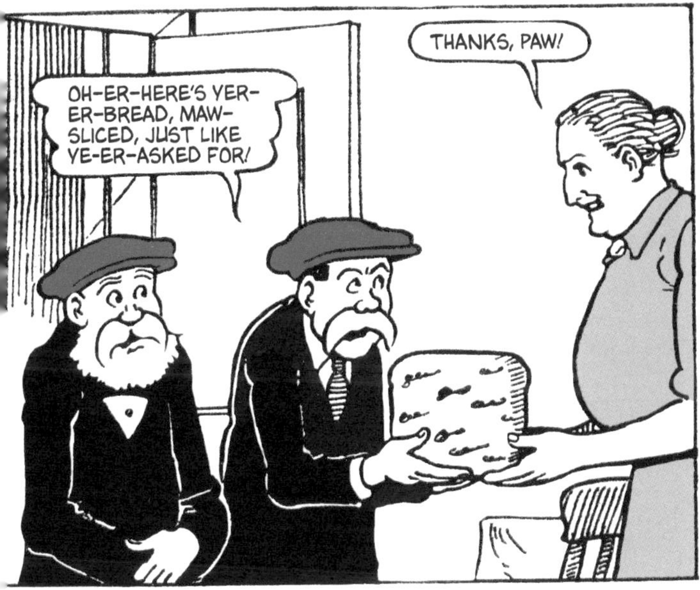
OH-ER-HERE'S YER-ER-BREAD, MAW-SLICED, JUST LIKE YE-ER-ASKED FOR!
THANKS, PAW!

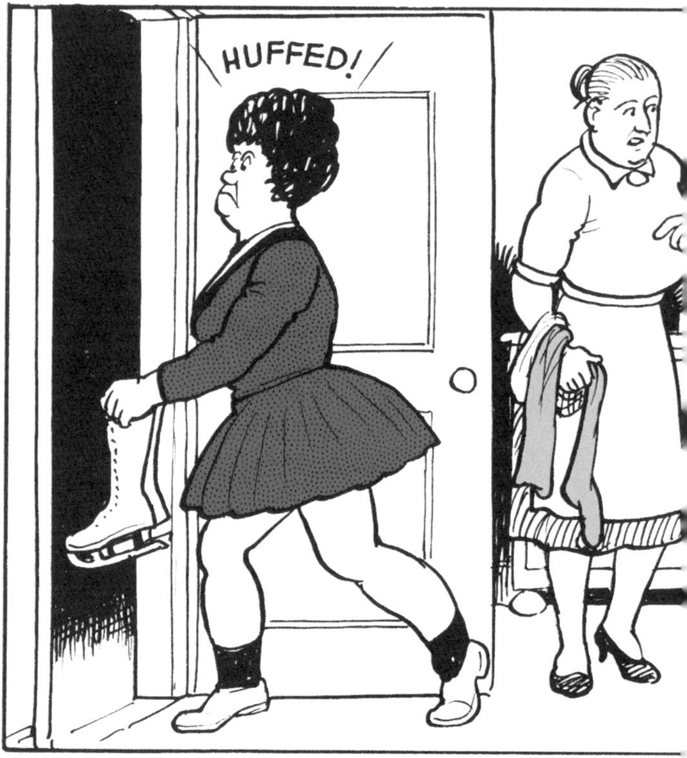
HUFFED!

The larger woman should always dress with dignity and decorum. However, in cases

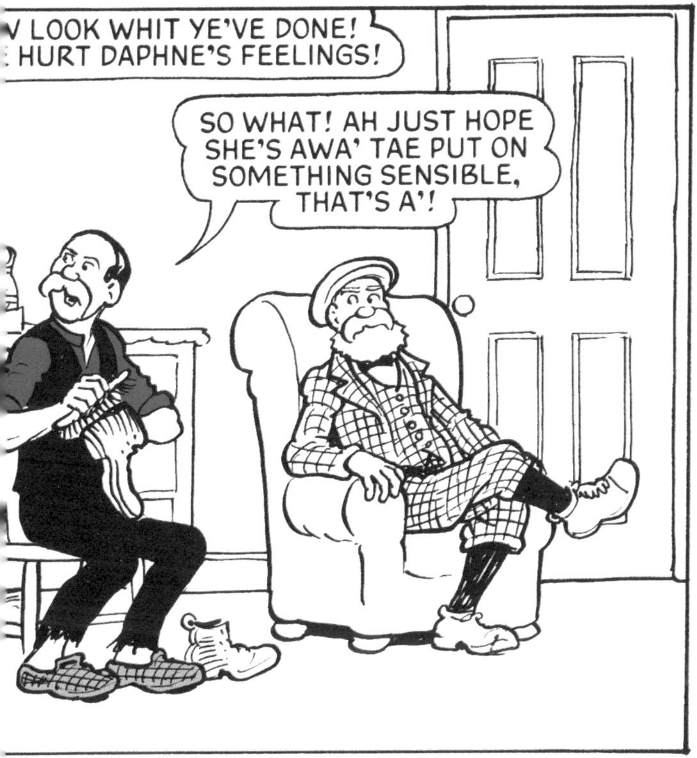
V LOOK WHIT YE'VE DONE!
: HURT DAPHNE'S FEELINGS!
SO WHAT! AH JUST HOPE SHE'S AWA' TAE PUT ON SOMETHING SENSIBLE, THAT'S A'!

where this rule of etiquette is not observed, personal remarks should be avoided.

Although the elderly may be annoying and frustrating at times, it is not good manners to use physical violence to keep them in check.

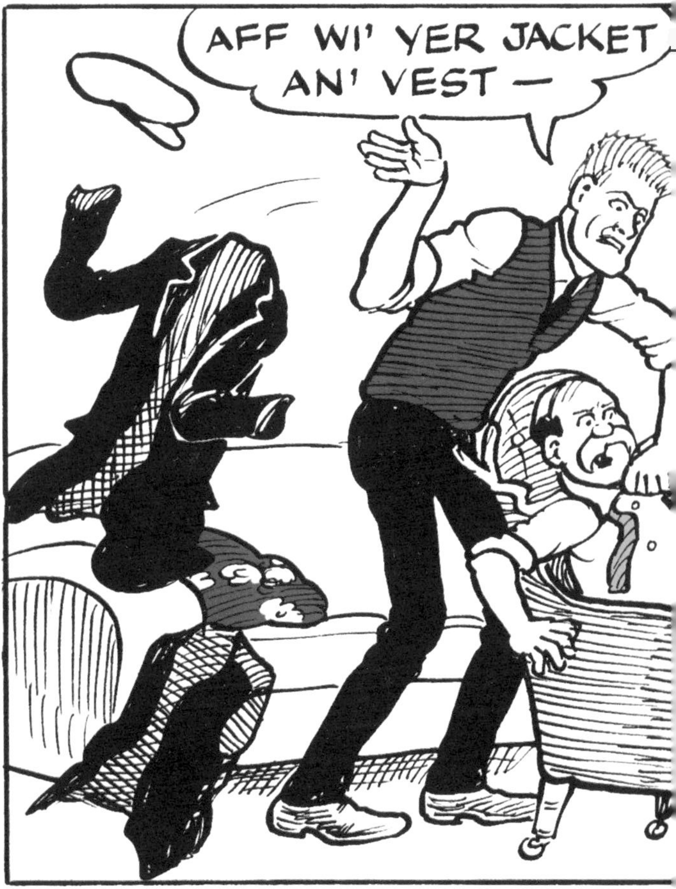
AFF WI' YER JACKET AN' VEST –

If a person does not wish to take part in The Auchenshoogle Dramatic Society's version

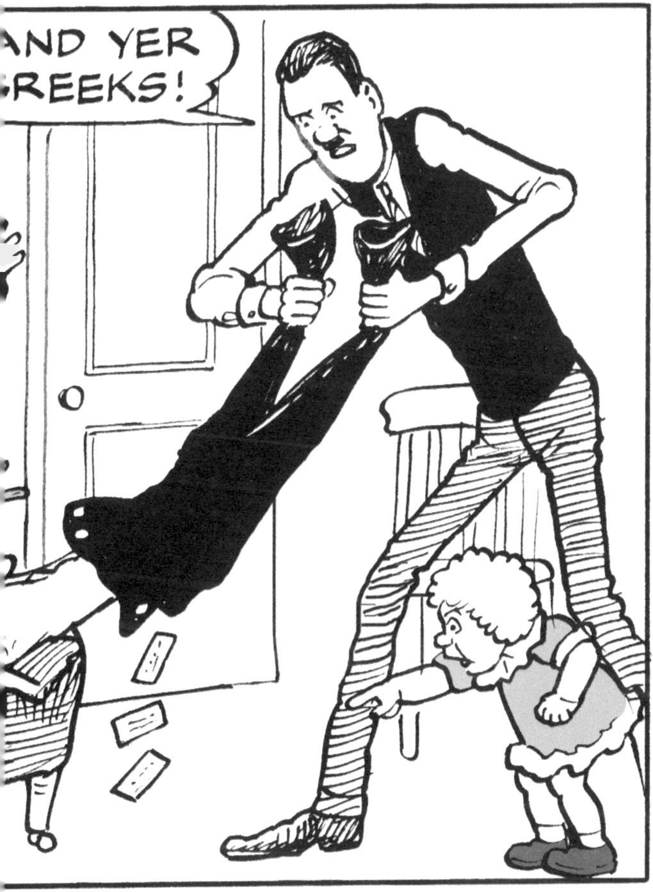
ND YER
REEKS!

of 'The Full Monty', it is only correct that their viewpoint be respected.

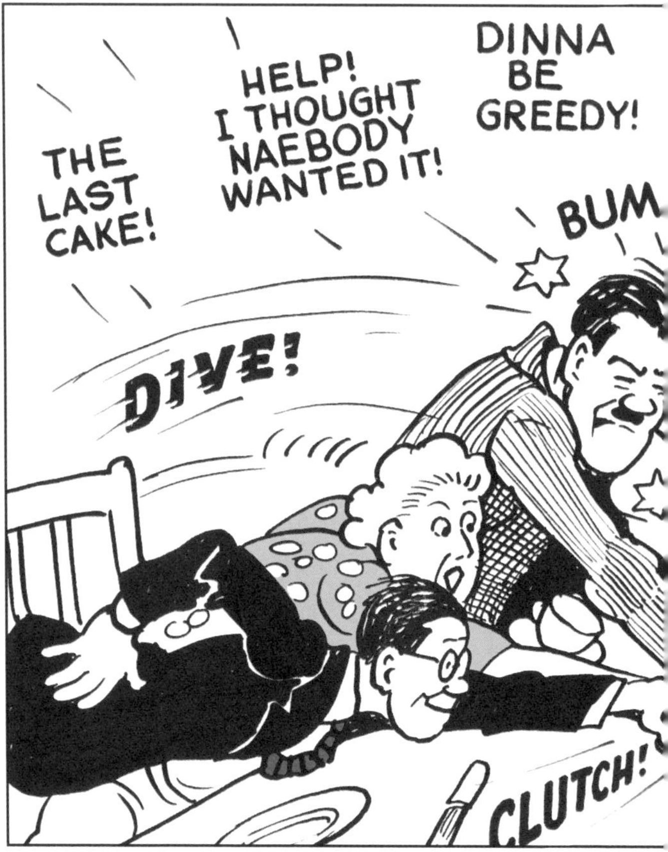
THE LAST CAKE!
HELP! I THOUGHT NAEBODY WANTED IT!
DINNA BE GREEDY!
BUM
DIVE!
CLUTCH!

During family games of snap, always use playing cards rather than cakes. So-called 'Patisserie Snap' can be

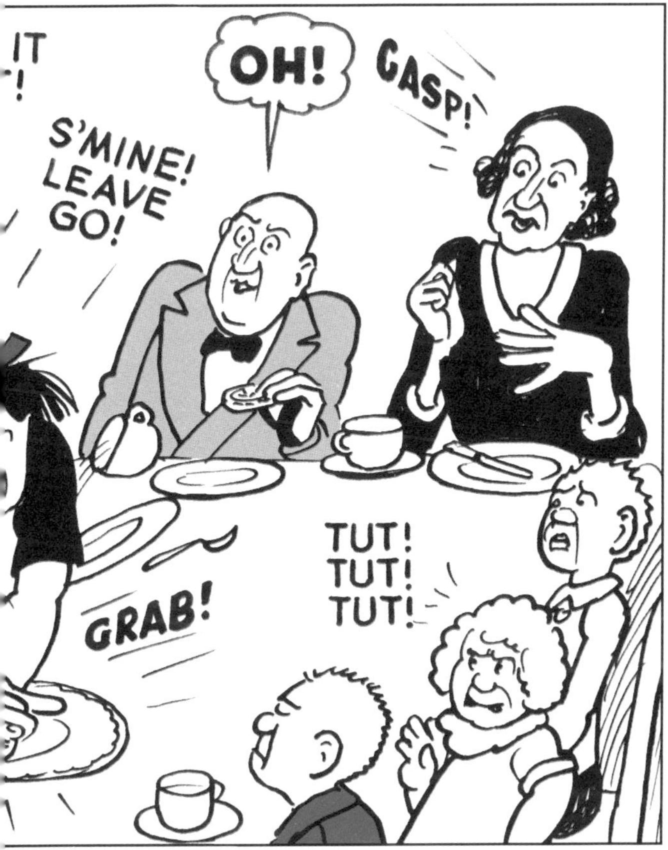
S'MINE! LEAVE GO!
OH!
GASP!
GRAB!
TUT! TUT! TUT!

extremely messy, dangerous and is an unacceptable waste of valuable bakery products.

When bathing, one should remove all clothing including headgear. Smoking during one's ablutions is also to be deplored as stray ash in the water may make one dirtier than when one got into the tub.

Though it may be amusing to see one's older sister careering down the street at twenty miles an hour, it is very bad etiquette to throw dangerous banana skins in front of anyone.

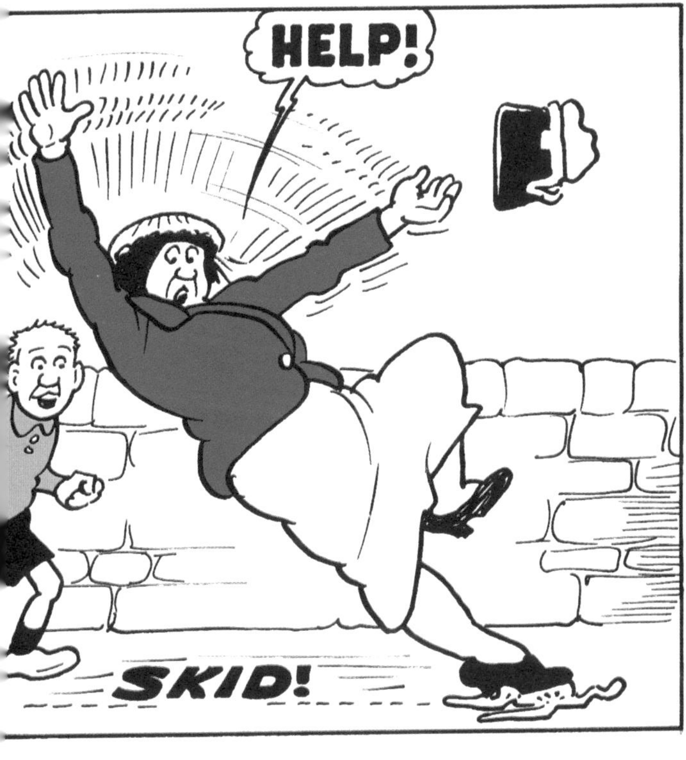
HELP!
SKID!

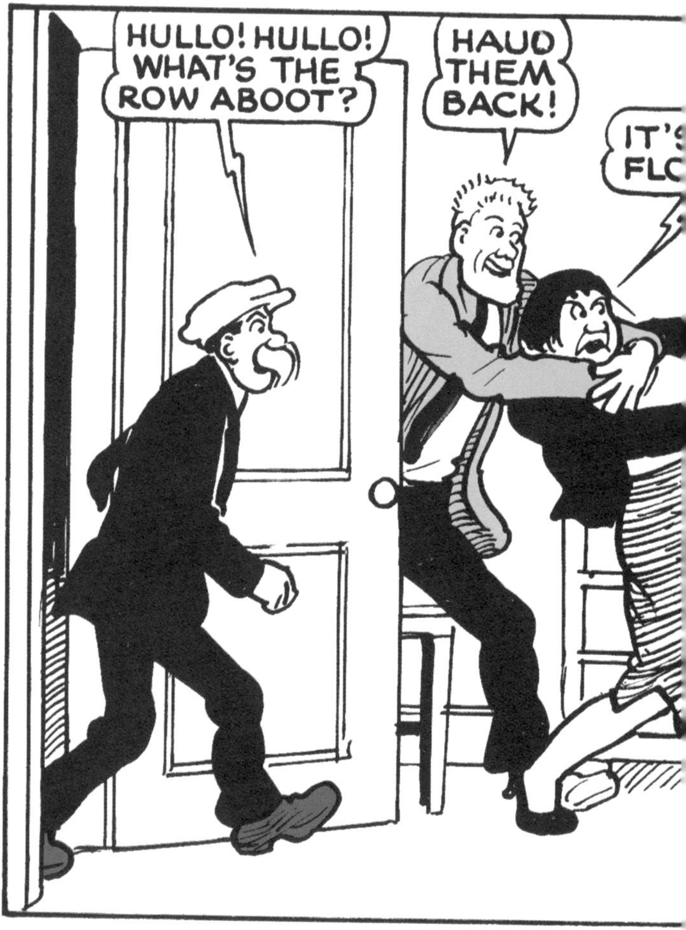
HULLO! HULLO! WHAT'S THE ROW ABOOT?
HAUD THEM BACK!

In polite society, petty squabbles about who caught the bride's bouquet should be

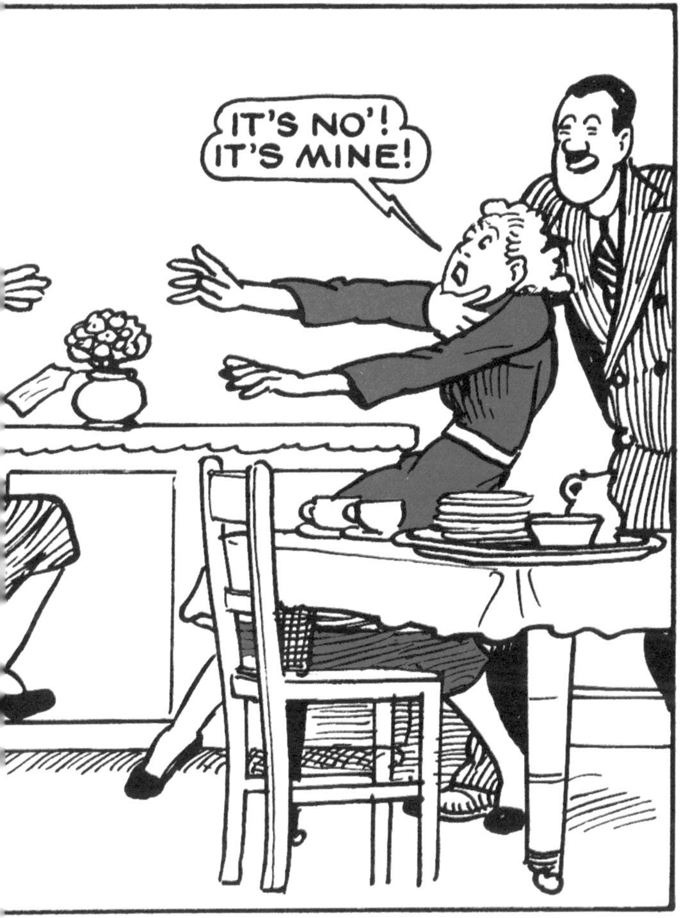
IT'S NO'! IT'S MINE!

settled amicably. Scrapping like wildcats is so undignified!

It is good etiquette to always fasten belts and buckles securely. It looks smart and tends to prevent unfortunate accidents. However, one should never say 'Belt up!' to an acquaintance.

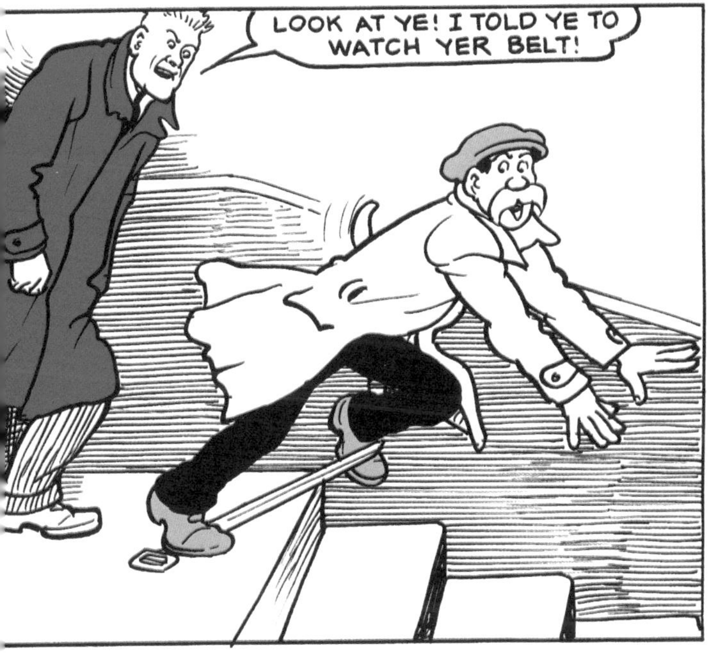
LOOK AT YE! I TOLD YE TO WATCH YER BELT!

Try to refrain from burping in public. This is vulgar, unpleasant and embarrassing. If such a thing happens, always say 'I beg your pardon!' rather than 'It wisnae me!' Bean and pickle sandwiches for luncheon should be avoided.

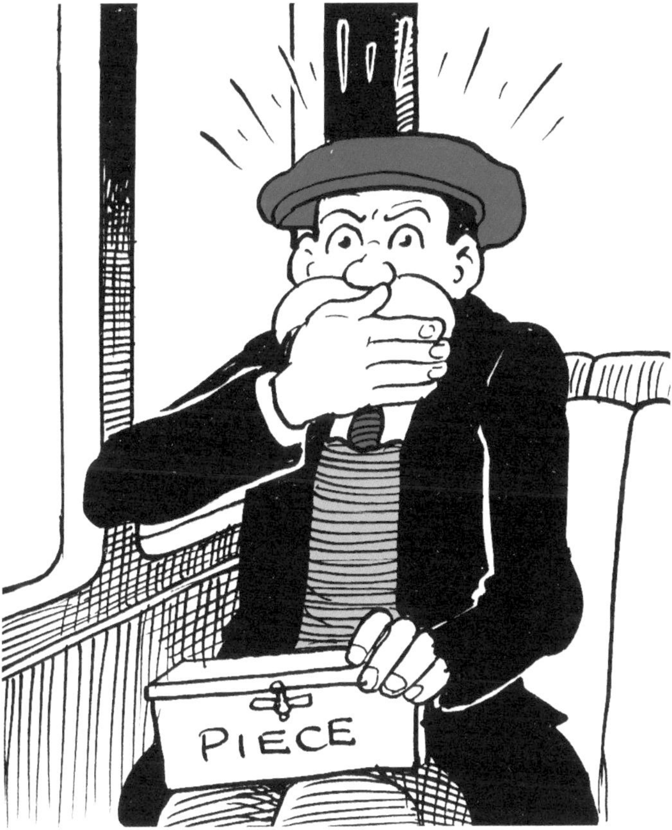
PIECE

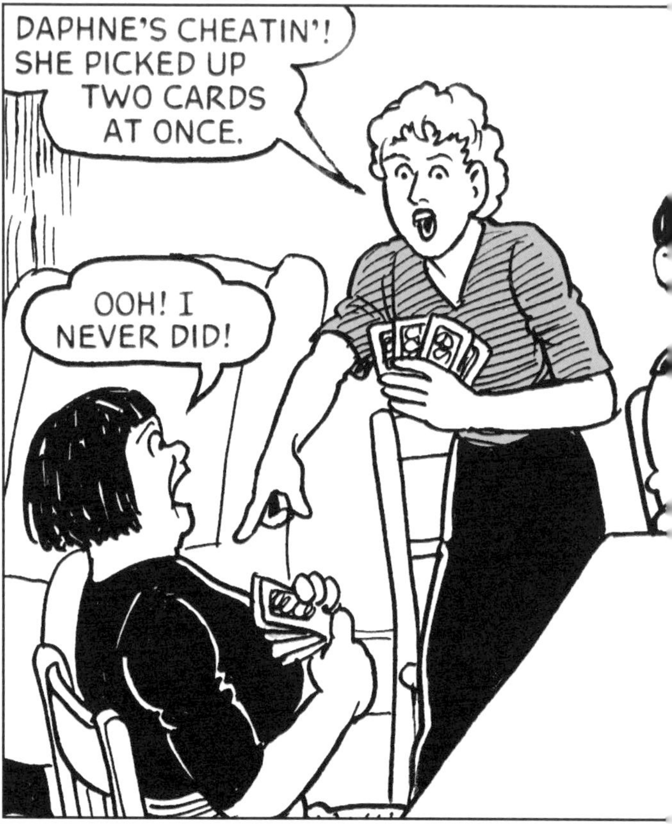
DAPHNE'S CHEATIN'! SHE PICKED UP TWO CARDS AT ONCE.
OOH! I NEVER DID!

Etiquette is particularly important in card games. One should never look at other players' cards, conceal cards

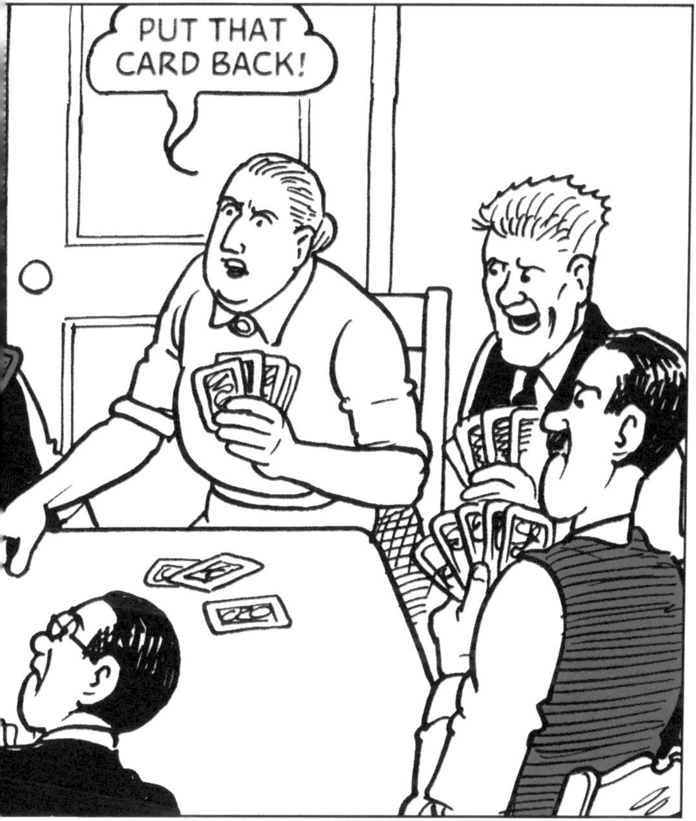
PUT THAT CARD BACK!

about your person, use speech play or call anyone a 'dirty, cheatin', lyin' galloot!'

If one's father is unable to provide you with a monetary loan, good manners dictate that you accept his difficult position. On no account should you turn him upside down to relieve him of his small change.

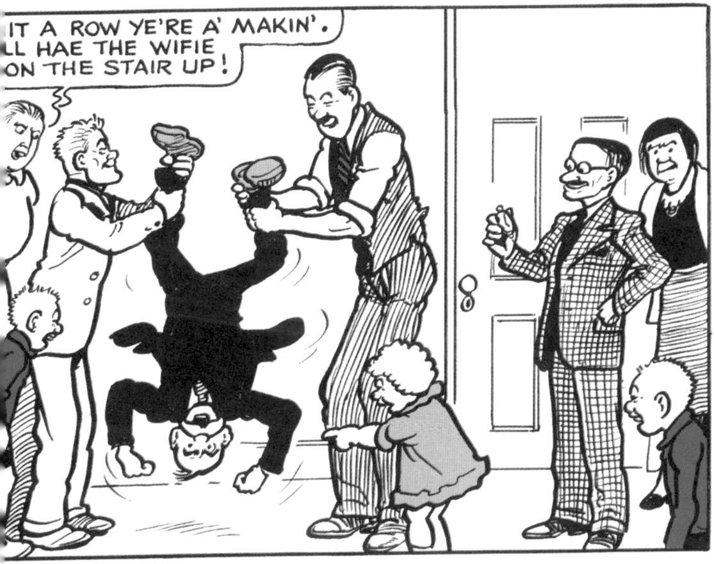
IT A ROW YE'RE A' MAKIN'.
LL HAE THE WIFIE
ON THE STAIR UP!

Horseplay and tomfoolery show one's manners in a very poor light. Such goings-on inevitably result in injury, damage and ghastly unpleasantness.

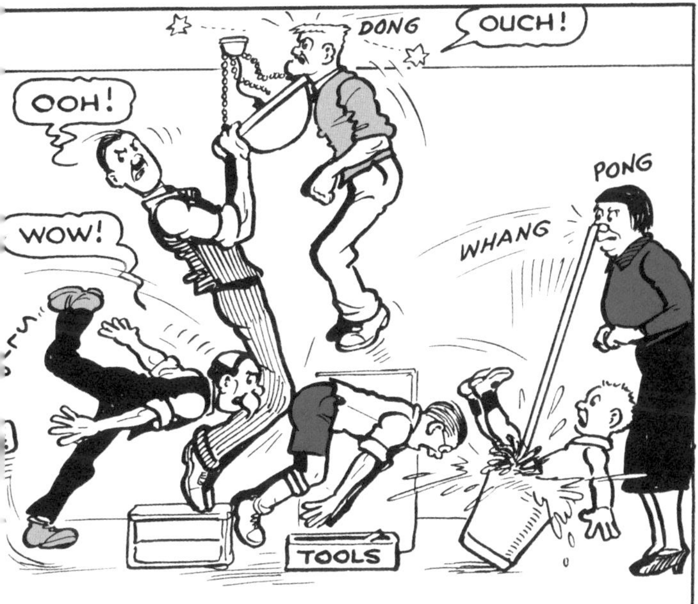
OOH!
DONG
OUCH!
WOW!
WHANG
PONG
TOOLS

Nowadays smoking is considered to be very bad manners. It has been suggested that one way to rid yourself of the filthy habit is to shoot the source of the problem and rid yourself of temptation once and for all.

MINUTES
ATER
RIFLE
SHOOTING 3D
TRY A SHOT
AND WIN A PRIZE
BANG

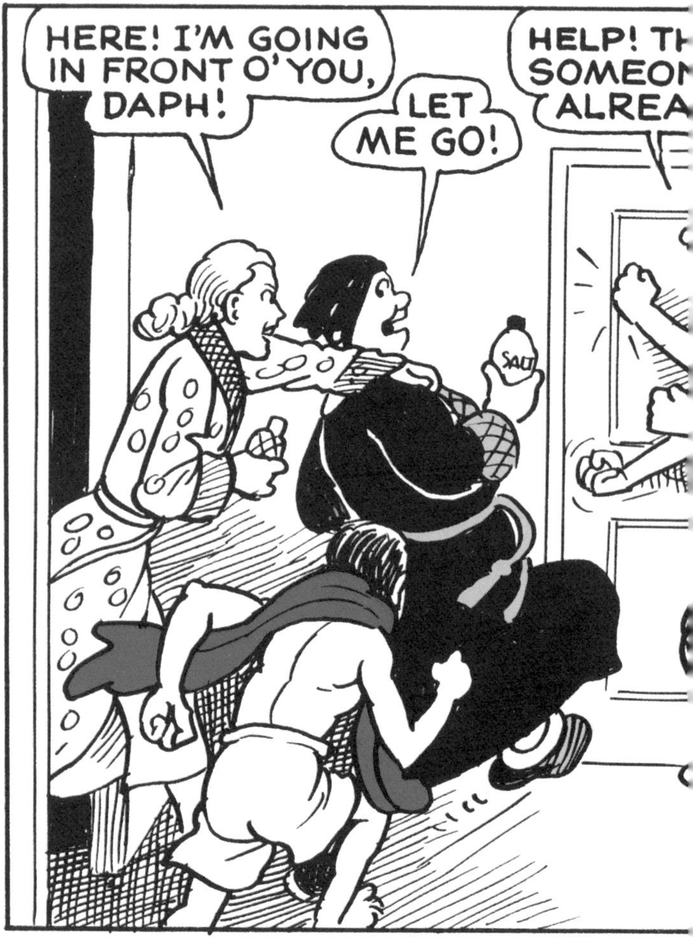
HERE! I'M GOING IN FRONT O' YOU, DAPH!
LET ME GO!
HELP!
SALT

After overdosing on Maw's Prune and Rhubarb Crumble, it is polite to form an orderly

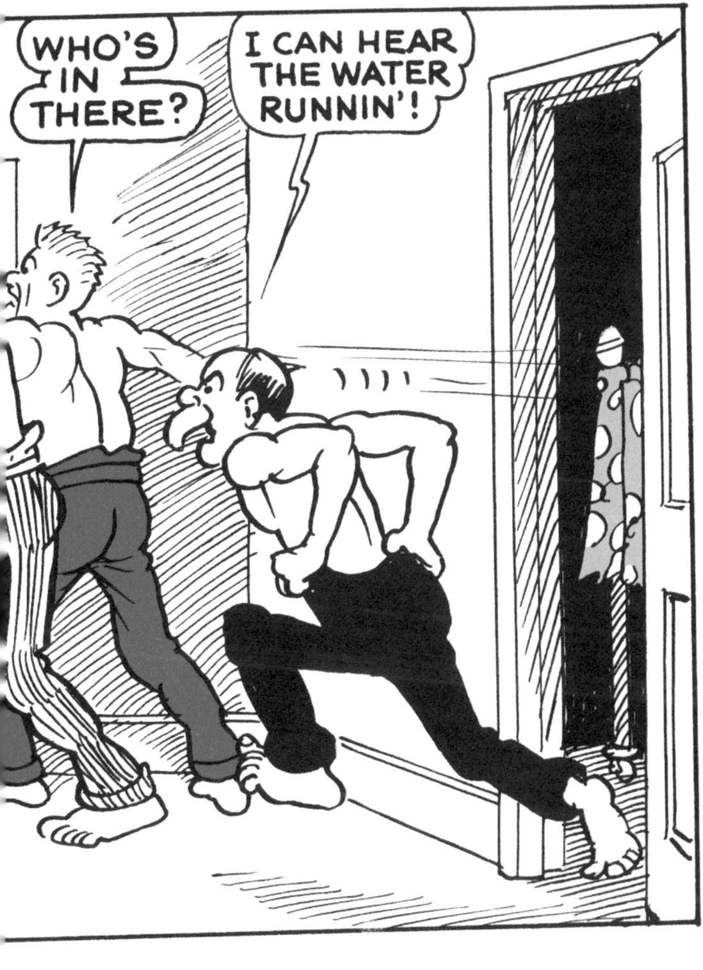
WHO'S IN THERE?
I CAN HEAR THE WATER RUNNIN'!

queue for the toilet facilities. An undignified stampede is decidedly unseemly.

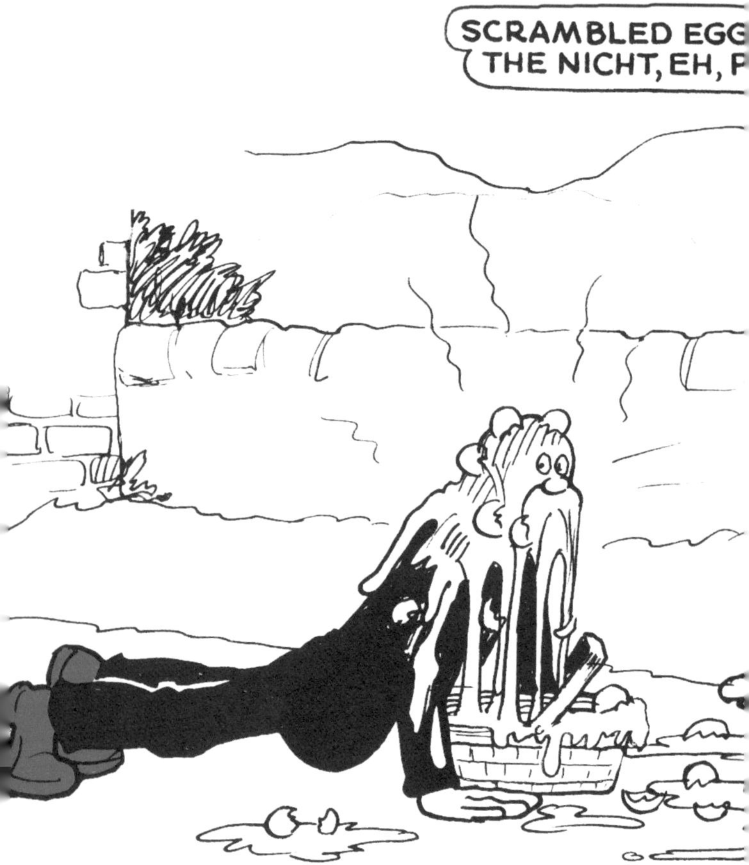
SCRAMBLED EGG
THE NICHT, EH, P

Egg shampoo is excellent for giving one's hair and whiskers added lustre. However, this

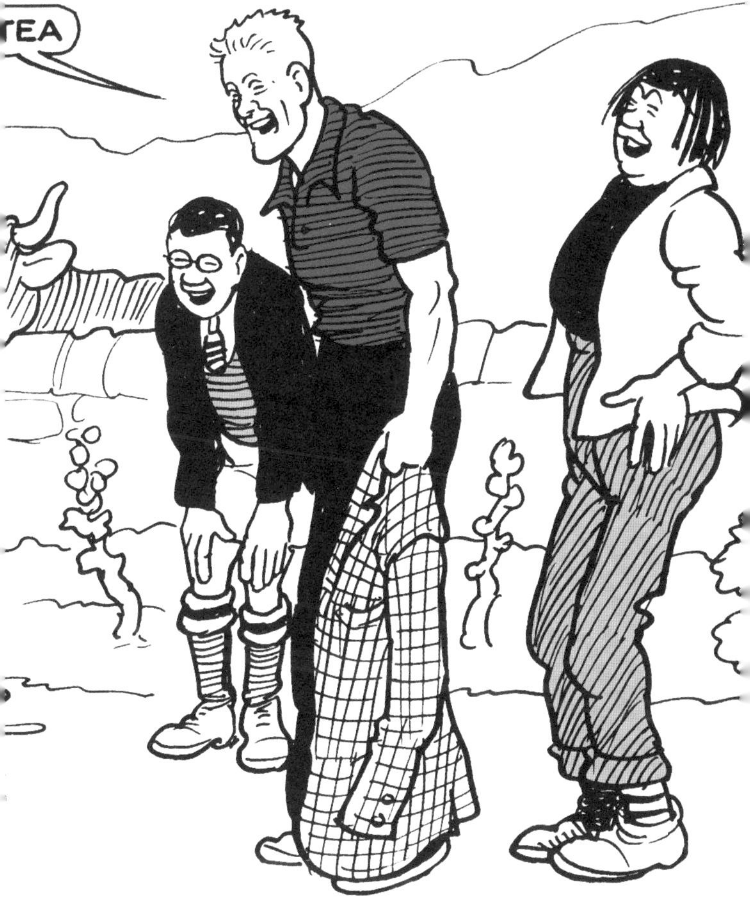
TEA

should be used in moderation and generally in the confines of one's bathroom.

In bygone days, Native Americans were said to have performed rain dances in times of drought. However, elderly pensioners doing the same thing in Auchenshoogle to try to boost their roses simply look ridiculous.

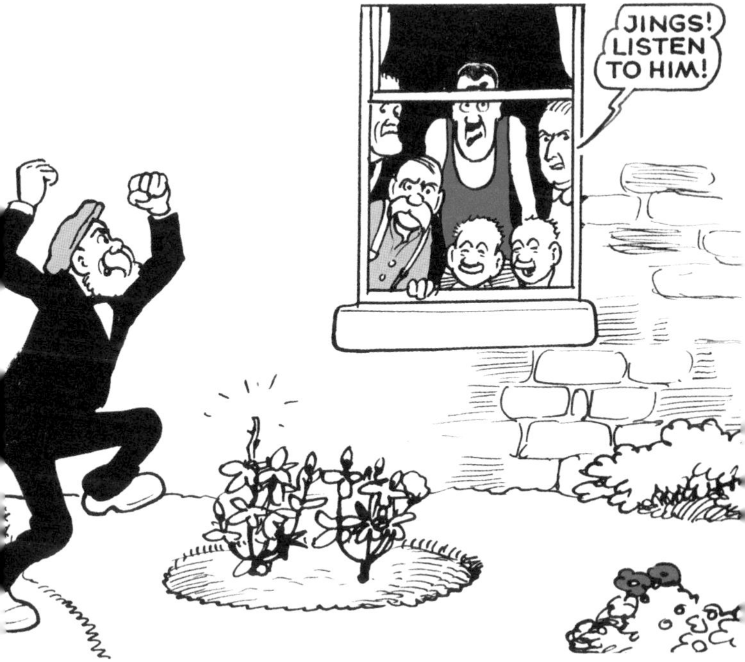
JINGS! LISTEN TO HIM!

Being smartly dressed is not necessarily the be all and end all in etiquette. If, for instance, your commitment to doing up your guest's tie crosses over into the territory of restricting his breath and blood flow, you have taken sartorial elegance too far.

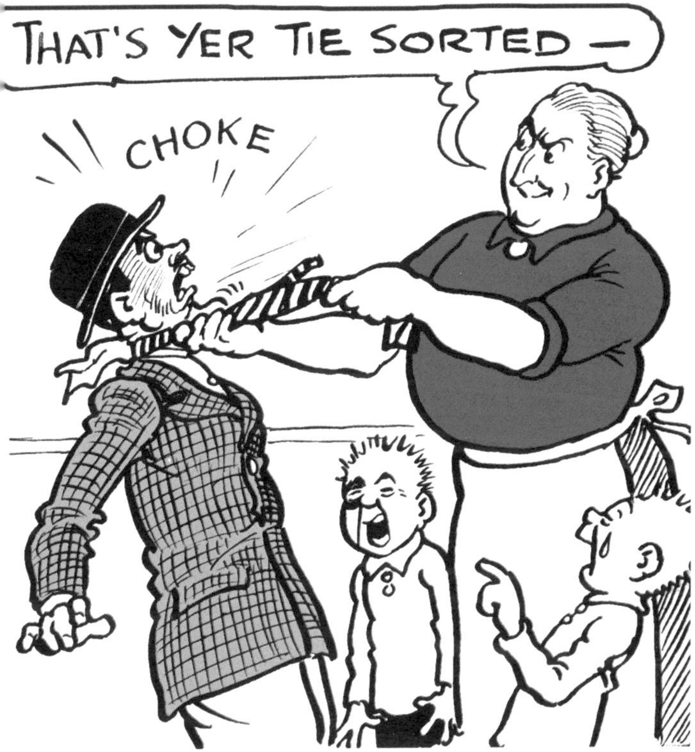
THAT'S YER TIE SORTED —
CHOKE

Sometimes guests will arrive unexpectedly and, while you might not always feel like entertaining, it is good manners to accommodate their visit with politeness and good grace.

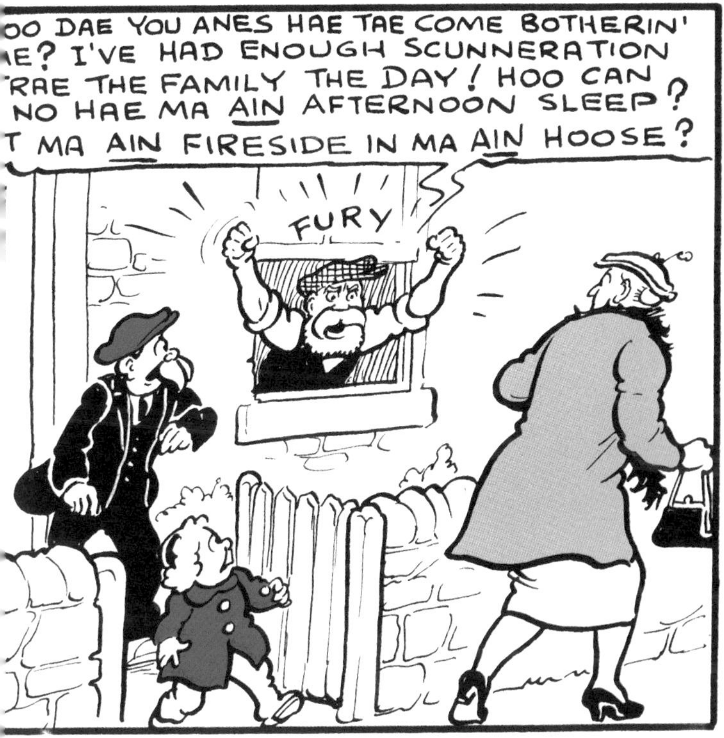
OO DAE YOU ANES HAE TAE COME BOTHERIN' ɅE? I'VE HAD ENOUGH SCUNNERATION 'RAE THE FAMILY THE DAY! HOO CAN NO HAE MA AIN AFTERNOON SLEEP? T MA AIN FIRESIDE IN MA AIN HOOSE?
FURY

If the rules and conventions of etiquette become too much to bear, then escape is the only option. But don't forget your bowler hat ...